All About America

GOLD RUSH AND RICHES

Paul Robert Walker

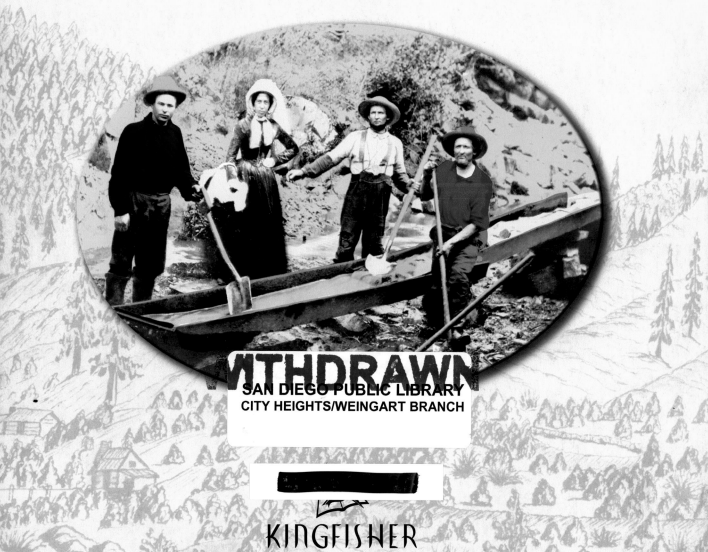

KINGFISHER
NEW YORK

KINGFISHER
LONDON & NEW YORK

Copyright © Bender Richardson White 2011

Published in the United States by Kingfisher,
175 Fifth Ave., New York, NY 10010
Kingfisher is an imprint of Macmillan Children's Books, London.
All rights reserved.

Distributed in the U.S. by Macmillan, 175 Fifth Ave.,
New York, NY 10010
Distributed in Canada by H.B. Fenn and Company Ltd.,
34 Nixon Road, Bolton, Ontario L7E 1W2

Library of Congress Cataloging-in-Publication data has been applied for.

ISBN paperback 978-0-7534-6512-7
ISBN reinforced library binding 978-0-7534-6584-4

Kingfisher books are available for special promotions and premiums. For details contact: Special Markets Department, Macmillan, 175 Fifth Ave., New York, NY 10010.

For more information, please visit www.kingfisherbooks.com

Printed in China
10 9 8 7 6 5 4 3 2 1
1TR/0311/WKT/UNTD/140MA

The All About America series was produced for Kingfisher by Bender Richardson White, Uxbridge, U.K.
Editor: Lionel Bender
Designer: Ben White
DTP: Neil Sutton
Production: Kim Richardson
Consultant: Richard Jensen, Research Professor of History, Culver Stockton College, Missouri

Sources of quotations and excerpts
Page 4, Marshall quote: Paul, Rodman W. *The California Gold Discovery*, p.118. Georgetown, CA: The Talisman Press, 1967.
Page 4, Marshall and Sutter: Bancroft, Hubert Howe. *The Works of Hubert Howe Bancroft: California Inter Pocula*, p.70. Whitefish, MT: Kessinger Publishing, 2007.
Page 6, Gold mania: Browning, Peter. *To the Golden Shore*, p. 48 (NY Herald, Dec. 11, 1848). Lafayette, CA: Great West Books, 1995.
Page 6, Gold fever: Walker, Paul Robert. *Trail of the Wild West*, p.16. National Geographic, 1997.
Page 8: Hester, Sallie. *"The Diary of a Pioneer Girl,"* April 27, 1849. In *Covered Wagon Women, Diaries & Letters from the Western Trails 1840–1890.* Volume I 1840–1849, p. 236. Edited and compiled by Kenneth L. Holmes. Glendale, CA: The Arthur H. Clark Company, 1983.
Page 13, Miner quote: Walker, Dale L. *Eldorado*, p. 262. New York: Tom Doherty Associates, 2003.
Page 18: Ramsay, Alexander. *"Alexander Ramsay's Gold Rush Diary of 1849,"* Sept. 21, 1849. Edited by Merrill J. Mattes. In *Pacific Historical Review*, Vol. XVIII, Nov. 1949, No. 4, p. 466.
Page 19, Gambling: Walker, Dale L. *Eldorado*, p. 308. New York: Tom Doherty Associates, 2003.
Page 27, Stampeder quote: Berton, Pierre. *Klondike*, p. 539. Revised edition. Toronto: Penguin Books, 1972.

Acknowledgments
The publishers would like to thank the following illustrators for their contribution to this book: Peter Dennis, Inklink Firenze, Nick Hewetson, John James, and Gerald Wood. Map: Neil Sutton. Book cover design: Michael Yuen.
Cover artwork: Shane Marsh (Linden Artists).
The publishers thank the following for supplying photos for this book: *b* = bottom, *c* = center, *l* = left, *t* = top, *m* = middle
© The Art Archive: page 20–21t (The Art Archive/Granger Collection) • © Getty Images: pages 4br (Peter Newark American Pictures); 5t (Getty Images); 11bl (SuperStock); 13t (Gallo Images-Denny Allen); 13bl (American School); 15 (American School); 24–25 (VisionsofAmerica/Joe Sohm); 26tr (Graham Coton); 26–27 (Archive Photos) • © istockphoto.com: pages 4t and cover (Dmitriy Norov); 10–11t (Duncan Walker); 12tl (Matthew Ragen); 12tr (pixhook); 13br (Tom Mc Nemar); 16r (Ron Bailey); 18tl (Pablo Caridad); 24tl (Caitlin Mirra); 25l (Eric Hood); 28tl (dgmata); 29t (Marcin Sadlowski) • © Library of Congress: (LC-DIG-ppmsc-04825) pages 1, 2–3, 30–31, 32; 18m (LC-USZC2-31); 26tl (LC-USZC4-8279) • © TopFoto.co.uk: The Granger Collection/TopFoto pages 4ml, 6, 7t, 7b, 8–9t, 9t, 9m, 9b, 10–11t and cover, 11m, 14, 14–15, 16l, 17l, 19bl, 20tl and cover, 20m, 21bl and cover, 21br, 22, 23t, 23b, 25tr, 26ml, 27tr, 28–29, 28b, 29b; 1 (Topfoto); 19br (ullsteinbild/TopFoto).
Every effort has been made to trace the copyright holders of the images. The publishers apologize for any omissions.

Note to readers: The website addresses listed in this book are correct at the time of publishing. However, due to the ever-changing nature of the Internet, website addresses and content can change. Websites can contain links that are unsuitable for children. The publisher cannot be held responsible for changes in website addresses or content, or for information obtained through third-party websites. We strongly advise that Internet searches should be supervised by an adult.

CONTENTS

Introduction

Gold Rush and Riches looks at the sudden rush of people to California and neighboring states starting in 1848, as gold and other precious metals were found there. It describes and illustrates how the miners arrived, searched for gold, worked their claims and, if they were lucky enough to find "rich diggings," spent their money. It also tells how many miners failed and returned home, and it relates the tales of those who found even greater riches by supplying the miners and offering other services in gold rush towns. The story is presented as a series of double-page articles, each one looking at a particular topic. It is illustrated with paintings, engravings, and photographs from the time, mixed with artists' impressions of everyday scenes and situations.

I Have Found It!

Flakes of gold spark a rush

Following a chance discovery, a gold rush took California by storm. With an announcement by the president, tens of thousands of Americans headed for California.

John Augustus Sutter left his family in Switzerland to seek his fortune in North America. In 1839, he reached California, which was then part of Mexico. The Mexican government gave him 225 square miles (583 sq km) of land to encourage other settlers. Sutter built a fort in what is now Sacramento, California, and began many projects with hundreds of American Indians working for him. He did not have enough wood, so he hired a carpenter named James Marshall to build a sawmill at Coloma on the American River. On January 24, 1848, Marshall found shiny flakes in a channel he was digging for the sawmill. "I have found it!" he said, showing the flakes to one of his workers. "What is it?" asked the worker. "Gold . . . I know it to be nothing else."

◀ In order to gain trust and borrow money, John Sutter called himself "Captain" and pretended he had been in the Swiss cavalry.

The Finest Kind of Gold

Four days after his discovery, Marshall (right) rode 40 miles (64 km) to Sutter's Fort in a driving rainstorm and showed Sutter the metal he had found. Together, they ran a series of tests and concluded that Marshall had found "the finest kind of gold."

Word Leaks Out

Sutter and Marshall tried to keep the discovery a secret because Sutter was afraid that his dreams of a California empire would be destroyed if thousands of gold seekers swarmed over the land. He turned out to be correct, but the secret could not be kept for long. His workers began to desert, and by March 1848, a group of men had found richer "diggings" down the river from Coloma. That was just the beginning of the California gold rush.

▶ This diary entry by Henry Bigler, one of the millworkers, records the discovery of gold by James Marshall.

◀ Coloma lies in a beautiful valley on the South Fork of the American River.

◀ At Sutter's Mill, water flowed through a channel to turn a big wheel, which powered the saw blade. It was in the back of the channel, called the tailrace, that James Marshall discovered gold.

▼ The main mining regions of the western United States in the 1800s

CANADA

Deadwood

Sacramento
Comstock Lode
Sutter's Mill
Salt Lake City
San Francisco

Denver
Leadville

Los Angeles

Tombstone

N

MEXICO

| Gold |
| Silver |
| Gold & Silver |

Gold! Gold! Gold!

On May 8, 1848, a man named Sam Brannan—who owned a store at Sutter's Fort—stepped onto the wharf in San Francisco and held a small bottle for everyone to see, shouting, "Gold! Gold! Gold from the American River!" By the end of the month, San Francisco was almost empty, as the citizens headed up the Sacramento River to the American River and the goldfields. Sam Brannan's store took in $36,000 (about $1 million by today's value) in gold in ten weeks, selling supplies to the gold seekers. Brannan went on to become California's first millionaire.

The gold seekers soon discovered that gold could be found in almost every river, stream, and gulch on the western slopes of the Sierra Nevada. Word traveled slowly to the East, where most people considered the stories of gold to be an exaggeration. That all changed greatly on December 5, 1848, when President James K. Polk announced that the stories were true. Two days later, a large container arrived from California with 230 ounces (6.5 kg) of extremely pure gold. The rush was on!

The News Is Out!

The rush to California begins

Gold fever spread throughout the country, and some 80,000 people left their old lives to follow the call of gold. The first eastern gold seekers traveled to California by sea, either sailing around South America or crossing Panama. San Francisco became a boomtown.

At the time of the gold discovery, there were around 14,000 non–American Indian people in California. They were mostly a mix of Mexican "Californios" and American settlers. By the end of the year, another 6,000 had arrived, drawn by the promise of gold. These early arrivals came from such places in the west as the Sandwich Islands (Hawaii), Oregon, Mexico, Peru, and Chile. Once word reached the Mississippi Valley and the East Coast, this small stream of miners turned into a flood. In 1849 alone, 80,000 gold seekers—who called themselves forty-niners—headed for California. All across the nation farmers and storekeepers gave up their jobs. A New York paper proclaimed: "The gold mania rages with intense vigor, and is carrying off its victims hourly and daily." Many people on the East Coast headed to California by sea, while those who lived farther west traveled overland.

Coleman's California Line,
FOR SAN FRANCISCO,
SAILING REGULARLY AS ADVERTISED
Clipper of SATURDAY, March 17th.

THE MAGNIFICENT EXTREME CLIPPER SHIP

STORM KING

CALLAGHAN, Commander,

Is now rapidly Loading at Pier 15 East River.

This celebrated Vessel is well known to the trade as an EXTREME CLIPPER, and her uniform rapid passages and excellent delivery of cargo, render her at once

THE POPULAR SHIP OF THE PORT,

and insures her speedy dispatch, as above. She rates Ai fully first class, and insures at the lowest rates.

WM. T. COLEMAN & CO., 88 Wall St.,
Tontine Building.

Agents in San Francisco, Messrs. WM. T. COLEMAN & CO.

◄ Advertisement for a clipper ship

▼ Almost half of the gold seekers came to California by sea. The journey was long, hard, and dangerous.

Around the Horn

The main sea route from New York to San Francisco was around the coast of South America, through the stormy waters off Cape Horn. The 13,600-mile (21,900-km) voyage normally took about six months, but a gold seeker with money could board a fast clipper ship and make the journey in four months.

The first ships fill the harbor

The first gold seekers to travel by sea from the East Coast arrived on February 28, 1849—13 months after the great discovery. They traveled a brand-new route: by steamboat from New York to Panama at the southern tip of Central America, across a narrow strip of land called an isthmus, and then by another steamboat along the West Coast to San Francisco. (The Panama Canal was not built until 1914.) It was faster than the old route around Cape Horn, but the jungles of Panama were infested with disease-carrying insects and were hard to travel through.

AN ACCOUNT OF

CALIFORNIA,

AND THE

WONDERFUL GOLD REGIONS.

A New Arrival at the Gold Diggings.

WITH A DESCRIPTION OF

The Different Routes to California;

Information about the Country, and the Ancient and Modern Discoveries of Gold;

How to Test Precious Metals; Accounts of Gold Hunters;

TOGETHER WITH MUCH OTHER

Useful Reading for those going to California, or having Friends there.

ILLUSTRATED WITH MAPS AND ENGRAVINGS.

BOSTON:

PUBLISHED BY J. B. HALL, 66 CORNHILL.

For Sale at Skinner's Publication Rooms, 6

Price 12½ cents.

The First Boomtown in the West

At the time of the gold discovery, San Francisco was a village of less than 1,000 people. When the big ships began to arrive in the summer of 1849, it grew to 5,000. A year later, it had a population of 30,000. Some of the ships were dragged ashore and used as buildings.

GUNS, PISTOLS, AMMUNITION, HARDWARE, TINWARE.

THE BANK

LIQUOR STORE

SALOON

HOTEL

GENERAL STORE

◀ In this 1850 painting, a group of New Yorkers talk excitedly about the latest news from California.

Gold Fever

After a U.S. Army sergeant first saw gold, he wrote: "A frenzy seized my soul . . . Piles of gold rose up before me at every step; castles of marble dazzling the eye . . . in short, I had a very violent attack of gold fever."

Golden rivers

Many rivers flow down from the towering peaks of the Sierra Nevada and pour into California's two largest rivers—the Sacramento and the San Joaquin. Over millions of years, these smaller rivers carried gold, quartz, and other minerals down from the mountains, where it was found by the California gold seekers—sometimes in the river itself, sometimes in a stream, and sometimes in a dry gulch or other area where a river had once run.

California Ho!

The overland journey to the goldfields

The restless settlers of the Mississippi and Ohio valleys traveled to California by land, in covered wagons, on horses and mules, and even on foot. It was a long and dangerous journey across plains, mountains, and deserts.

The most popular overland route to California followed the well-worn Oregon Trail along the Platte River in Nebraska; crossed the Rocky Mountains at South Pass in Wyoming; and then broke off for California, either at South Pass or farther west, at Fort Hall in Idaho. In the spring of 1849, 35,000 California-bound travelers, called emigrants, gathered near towns on the Missouri River in Missouri and Iowa, preparing to make the journey of more than 2,000 miles (3,200 km). One of the emigrants, a 14-year-old girl named Sallie Hester, wrote in her diary, "As far as eye can reach, so great is the migration, you see nothing but wagons . . . a vast army on wheels."

▶ A guide describing the overland journey to California, first published in 1849

▼ In the first great migration of 1849, only a few women and children joined their husbands and fathers.

EMI

CA

CONTAININ
THE EMIG
WATER,
PASSES,
ROUTES,
WITH
ASS

BY

PUBLISH
N
S T

◀ The first part of the journey along the Platte River was fairly flat, but when the emigrants reached the mountains, they struggled to get their wagons over the rough terrain.

▼ Crossing the mountains

GUIDE
IA,
ORMATION FO[
S, DISTANCE[
G OF RIVE[
GE MAP[
TRY, &C[
TING A[
ORES.

ARE

SALL,

The Race West

Although emigrants felt they were racing each other to grab their share of gold, the real race during the journey was with the weather. In the spring, they had to wait until grass for their animals had grown on the plains. Yet they had to cross the Sierra Nevada before the mountain passes were snowbound.

For CALIFORNIA DIRECT this side up WITH CARE.

For CALIFORNIA DIRECT this side up WITH CARE.

▲ This cartoon captured the exciting energy of the gold rush, as men left their families behind to search for riches in California.

Dangers of the trail

The greatest danger in the journey along the Platte River was cholera, a deadly disease that killed many thousands of emigrants, leaving a line of shallow graves along the trail. Cholera disappeared when they reached the mountains, but then there was "mountain fever," and daily travel was harder and more backbreaking than it had been on the plains. Although the travelers feared the American Indians, there were few attacks. The worst part of the journey was across the deserts of Nevada, where dust burned their eyes, bad water made them sick, and horses and oxen died on the trail. After making it across the desert, the emigrants still had to cross the towering Sierra Nevada.

▲ Another cartoon showed a giant rubber band that stretched from the Atlantic to the Pacific oceans. When it was cut in the East, it would supposedly carry the travelers all the way to California!

Setting Up as a Miner
Getting supplied and outfitted

The forty-niners needed basic supplies for mining and for daily life in the wilderness. Many did not understand what they would need until they reached California, so goods bought in the East often proved useless at the mines.

Merchants made more money than all but the luckiest miners. In the East, storekeepers offered crazy products such as "goldometers" that were supposed to point to the gold and "California Gold Grease" that promised to pick up gold if you rubbed it on your body and rolled down a hill! Although some forty-niners did buy products they needed in the East, most had to buy their supplies in San Francisco or Sutter's Fort, where prices were very high. A common mining pan that cost 20¢ ($5.60 today) in the East cost $8 to $16 ($224 to $448 today) in Sam Brannan's store at Sutter's Fort.

What a Well-Stocked Forty-niner Needed

The basic items for a miner's "kit" or supplies were a shovel, pick, mining pan, blankets, tent, salt pork (bacon) or beef jerky, beans, flour, sugar, tea, and coffee. Other items that were good to have included a lamp, a kettle, a baking pan, an ax, a hatchet, a hoe, a pail, and a simple mining machine called a rocker or cradle. The mining pan would double as a dish for cooking and eating.

◀ **A miner buys supplies at a general store in San Francisco before heading out to the diggings.**

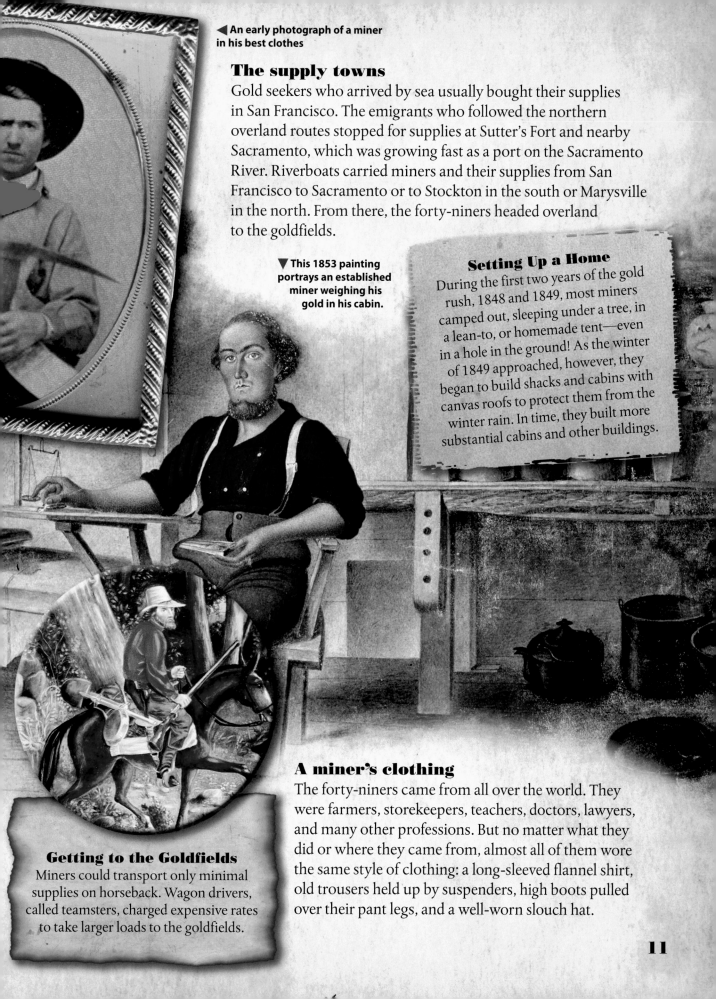

◀ An early photograph of a miner in his best clothes

The supply towns

Gold seekers who arrived by sea usually bought their supplies in San Francisco. The emigrants who followed the northern overland routes stopped for supplies at Sutter's Fort and nearby Sacramento, which was growing fast as a port on the Sacramento River. Riverboats carried miners and their supplies from San Francisco to Sacramento or to Stockton in the south or Marysville in the north. From there, the forty-niners headed overland to the goldfields.

▼ This 1853 painting portrays an established miner weighing his gold in his cabin.

Setting Up a Home

During the first two years of the gold rush, 1848 and 1849, most miners camped out, sleeping under a tree, in a lean-to, or homemade tent—even in a hole in the ground! As the winter of 1849 approached, however, they began to build shacks and cabins with canvas roofs to protect them from the winter rain. In time, they built more substantial cabins and other buildings.

Getting to the Goldfields

Miners could transport only minimal supplies on horseback. Wagon drivers, called teamsters, charged expensive rates to take larger loads to the goldfields.

A miner's clothing

The forty-niners came from all over the world. They were farmers, storekeepers, teachers, doctors, lawyers, and many other professions. But no matter what they did or where they came from, almost all of them wore the same style of clothing: a long-sleeved flannel shirt, old trousers held up by suspenders, high boots pulled over their pant legs, and a well-worn slouch hat.

Digging for Gold

A hard day's work

The forty-niners headed for California with dreams of riches, but they soon discovered that gold mining was hard work and most of the easily mined gold near the surface had been removed.

In the early days of the rush, there were stories of men prying gold out of a rock with a jackknife! The daily reality of gold mining was much more difficult. The basic concept was to wash gold-bearing "dirt" to separate the heavier gold from the soil, sand, and rocks. The simplest form of washing was to use a pan, but that was a slow, one-man operation. A small machine called a rocker or cradle allowed three men working together to process much more dirt. One man dug, another carried the dirt to the rocker, and the third washed the dirt.

A larger machine called a long tom allowed six to eight men to process ten times as much dirt as a rocker. The rocker and the long tom both operated on the same idea: With water rushing through the machine, dirt passed through a sieve that kept out large rocks and, at the bottom, flowed over ridges —called cleats or riffles—that trapped the heavier gold.

▶ **A pick helped the miner loosen hard dirt.**

▼ **The basic long tom was a single wooden trough about 10 feet (3 m) long. The long tom shown here has been extended with the hope of catching more gold.**

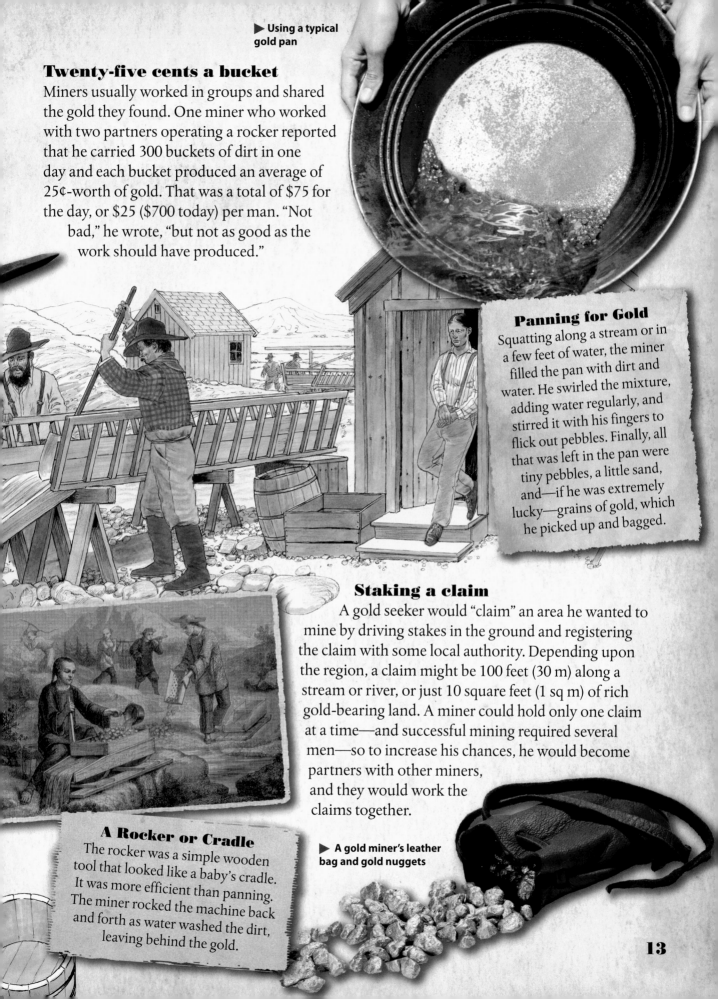

Twenty-five cents a bucket

Miners usually worked in groups and shared the gold they found. One miner who worked with two partners operating a rocker reported that he carried 300 buckets of dirt in one day and each bucket produced an average of 25¢-worth of gold. That was a total of $75 for the day, or $25 ($700 today) per man. "Not bad," he wrote, "but not as good as the work should have produced."

Panning for Gold

Squatting along a stream or in a few feet of water, the miner filled the pan with dirt and water. He swirled the mixture, adding water regularly, and stirred it with his fingers to flick out pebbles. Finally, all that was left in the pan were tiny pebbles, a little sand, and—if he was extremely lucky—grains of gold, which he picked up and bagged.

Staking a claim

A gold seeker would "claim" an area he wanted to mine by driving stakes in the ground and registering the claim with some local authority. Depending upon the region, a claim might be 100 feet (30 m) along a stream or river, or just 10 square feet (1 sq m) of rich gold-bearing land. A miner could hold only one claim at a time—and successful mining required several men—so to increase his chances, he would become partners with other miners, and they would work the claims together.

▶ A gold miner's leather bag and gold nuggets

A Rocker or Cradle

The rocker was a simple wooden tool that looked like a baby's cradle. It was more efficient than panning. The miner rocked the machine back and forth as water washed the dirt, leaving behind the gold.

The Goldfields

A mass of mines and people

The emigration of 1849 was only the beginning. Gold seekers kept coming to California until the gold that could be found easily by a small group of men was gone.

The California goldfields stretched for 200 miles (320 km) along the western slopes of the Sierra Nevada, from the Feather River in the north to the Mariposa River in the south. The area was around 60 miles (100 km) wide, a huge region holding potential riches. In the first year, 1848, perhaps 4,000 miners worked the rivers and "dry diggings" in old streambeds. About half of them were Californian American Indians, who did not know the value of gold and were employed and taken advantage of by the white miners. With the arrival of the forty-niners, the total number grew to 40,000. Many observers believed that 1852 marked the peak, with 100,000 miners working in the fields.

▲ The Chinese were the largest group of foreigners to head for California and stay. They called California *Gum Shan*, "Gold Mountain."

▲ This letter home from the mining town of Jacksonville, California, was sent in an envelope with an image of a miner.

▼ Miners took turns digging, working a rocker or long tom, and sifting through debris for gold.

The Mother Lode

Gold deposits had been created when the mountains were formed, when hot metals flowed into cracks in the rocks, forming "veins." Beginning north of Coloma and extending 120 miles (190 km) to the south was a huge vein between a few hundred feet and 2 miles (3 km) wide. Miners called it the Mother Lode. The mountains had eroded over millions of years, and the gold in this vein and other veins like it had been washed down to rivers and streams in the form of rocks, pebbles, and fine grains—to be found by the forty-niners.

A flash in the pan

With machines like the rocker and long tom used for daily mining, panning was mostly used to test a new area for gold or to capture small bits of gold that had been lost after going through the machines. Nothing excited a miner's heart like seeing a flash of bright gold in his pan.

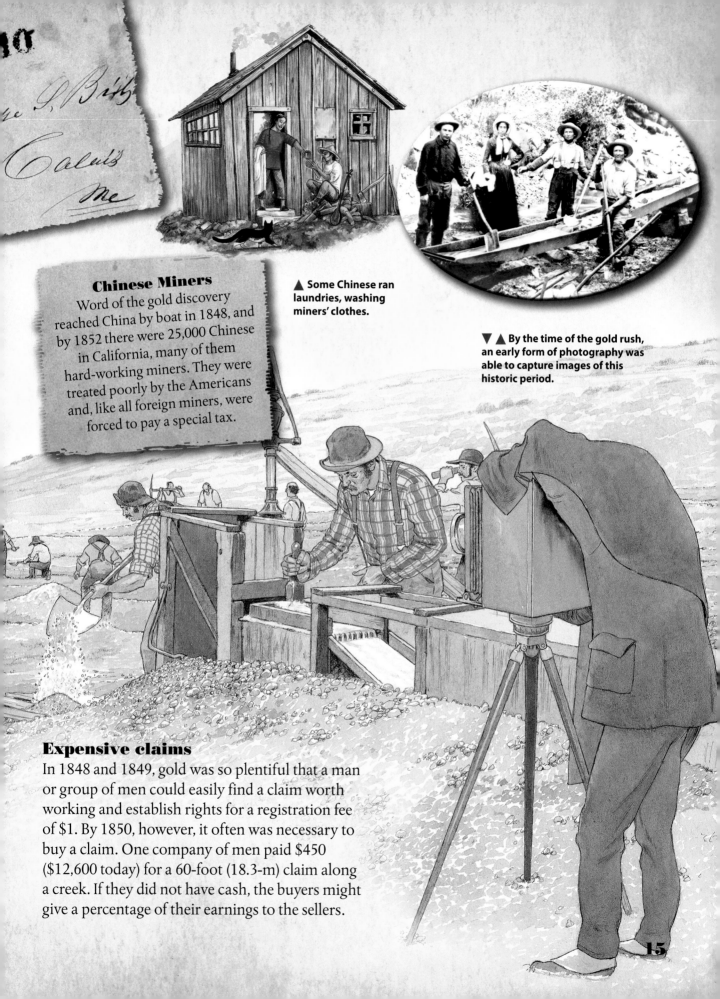

Chinese Miners

Word of the gold discovery reached China by boat in 1848, and by 1852 there were 25,000 Chinese in California, many of them hard-working miners. They were treated poorly by the Americans and, like all foreign miners, were forced to pay a special tax.

▲ Some Chinese ran laundries, washing miners' clothes.

▼▲ By the time of the gold rush, an early form of photography was able to capture images of this historic period.

Expensive claims

In 1848 and 1849, gold was so plentiful that a man or group of men could easily find a claim worth working and establish rights for a registration fee of $1. By 1850, however, it often was necessary to buy a claim. One company of men paid $450 ($12,600 today) for a 60-foot (18.3-m) claim along a creek. If they did not have cash, the buyers might give a percentage of their earnings to the sellers.

Striking Lucky
The California lottery

Gold miners were also called prospectors because they were always looking for the prospect or chance of gold.

Gold was scattered throughout the California gold region, but it was not everywhere. One claim might produce a small fortune, while a nearby claim produced little or nothing at all. A hard-working farmer from New York State named William Swain worked two claims on the Feather River, even building a dam with other men, but gave up after a year in California with only $500-worth of gold to show for his efforts. Yet a group of men working on the same river earned $8,000 each and sold their claims for $12,000 before heading home in high spirits. The miners called it the California lottery and, like any lottery, there were far more losers than winners.

Converting Gold to Cash

During the first years of the gold rush, raw gold was the main currency for most purchases, at the value of $16 ($448 today) per ounce (28.35 g). But as early as 1849, a private company began to mint gold coins that were accepted as currency, and in 1850, the U.S. government gave the company official status. The San Francisco Mint was opened in 1854.

◀ Miners weighed their gold on a simple scale to discover how much they had earned.

Assaying Gold

The purity of gold is measured in "fineness," with a fineness of 1,000 being pure gold with no other minerals. To determine purity, the gold has to be melted and tested in a complex chemical process. California gold was unusually pure, averaging about 850 fine in the Sierra Nevada and more than 900 in some areas.

▼ A scale like this would be found in an assay office.

The Pilgrim rejoiceth ober his "Pile."

◀ In this 1853 image, a miner rejoices over his luck at finding gold.

A daily wage

There were many stories of rich finds. One man was said to have found $2,900 of gold in a single pan! However, in 1849, the average miner considered one ounce of gold worth $16 to be a decent daily wage. The average value of gold from one bucket of dirt was 10¢, so a miner had to process 160 buckets to earn his daily wage. By 1850, as it became harder to find gold, the average daily wage dropped to $10, and it kept dropping each year. Considering the high prices in California, this was not much money, but it was better than a coal miner could earn back East, where wages were around $1 per day.

How much gold?

No one knows for sure how much gold came out of California. Historians estimate that almost $650 million in gold ($18.2 billion in today's value) was mined between 1848 and 1860. The best year was 1852, when 100,000 miners dug out about $81 million in gold—the highest amount for one year in any gold rush. Although that sounds like a lot, it averaged only $810 per miner. And while some miners earned much more than that, most were lucky to earn their daily wages.

◀ A sluice was an extended long tom with more boxes and more cleats or riffles to catch the gold as the water washed the dirt down.

The Largest Nugget

In 1854, five men working an underground mine earned an ounce of gold per man a day. Then one of them stumbled on the largest nugget ever found in California: 195 pounds (88 kg), worth $43,534 ($1.22 million today).

◀ The sluice, long tom, and rocker all lost some gold in the process, so a miner often panned for the "tailings" that were lost.

Spending a Fortune

Easy come, easy go

In a world where a man could get rich by a single lucky find, there were plenty of opportunities to lose his wealth as fast as he found it.

Most miners were young, single men and, after working hard all week, they would look for some fun on a Saturday night or Sunday afternoon. Small towns, sometimes just a collection of tents, sprouted near the goldfields to offer entertainment—and a chance to lose their hard-won gold. A glass of whiskey cost a "pinch" of gold dust, but it was hard to say how big the pinch should be, and there was usually gambling, too. A miner who had a successful season might go to San Francisco, where a pretty lady would sit with him while he gambled for an ounce of gold an evening.

Bad, expensive food

Food was terrible in the goldfields—mostly rancid bacon, beans, and old beef jerky. It was almost as bad, and very expensive, in the small towns. One miner dug $5-worth of gold in a day and wrote, "If I had been a hearty eater, I could have eaten the value of my five dollars during the day."

▶ Ginger brandy was thought to be a "healthy" drink.

DR. C. V. GIRARD'S GINGER BRANDY.

A CERTAIN CURE for Cholera Colic Cramps Dysentery, Chills & Fever, is a delightful & healthy beverage.

FOR SALE HERE.

Chinese Restaurants

Along with gold mining, Chinese people established other businesses, including restaurants. At first these were mainly for Chinese workers because the white miners were prejudiced against the Chinese. In time, however, the tasty food became popular with people of all races. Today, San Francisco has the largest "Chinatown" outside of Asia, with many Chinese restaurants.

▶ Chinese restaurants became popular with white patrons as well as with the Chinese.

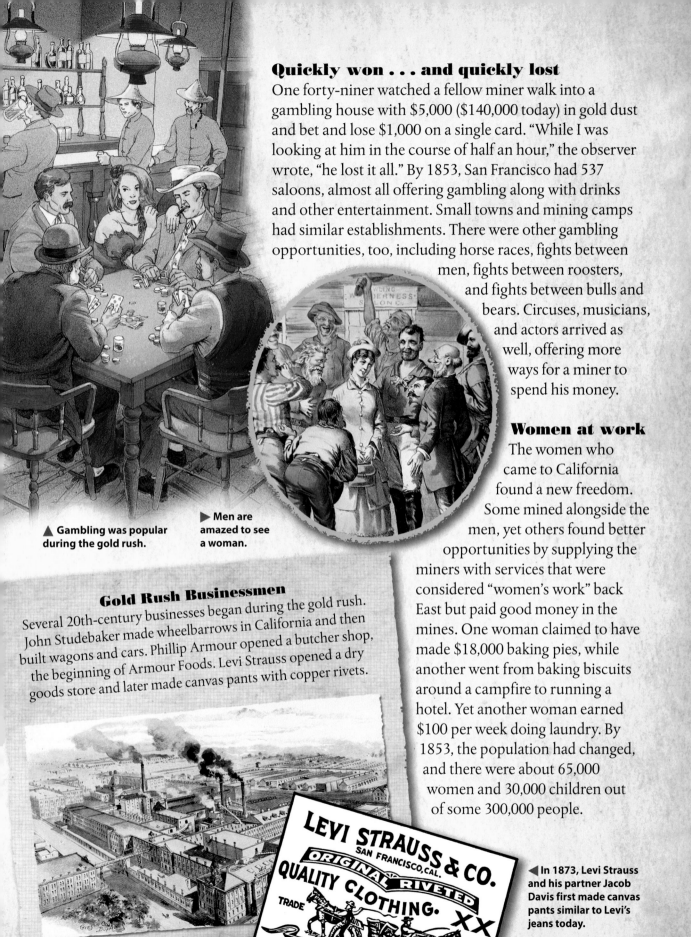

Quickly won . . . and quickly lost

One forty-niner watched a fellow miner walk into a gambling house with $5,000 ($140,000 today) in gold dust and bet and lose $1,000 on a single card. "While I was looking at him in the course of half an hour," the observer wrote, "he lost it all." By 1853, San Francisco had 537 saloons, almost all offering gambling along with drinks and other entertainment. Small towns and mining camps had similar establishments. There were other gambling opportunities, too, including horse races, fights between men, fights between roosters, and fights between bulls and bears. Circuses, musicians, and actors arrived as well, offering more ways for a miner to spend his money.

▲ Gambling was popular during the gold rush.

► Men are amazed to see a woman.

Women at work

The women who came to California found a new freedom. Some mined alongside the men, yet others found better opportunities by supplying the miners with services that were considered "women's work" back East but paid good money in the mines. One woman claimed to have made $18,000 baking pies, while another went from baking biscuits around a campfire to running a hotel. Yet another woman earned $100 per week doing laundry. By 1853, the population had changed, and there were about 65,000 women and 30,000 children out of some 300,000 people.

Gold Rush Businessmen

Several 20th-century businesses began during the gold rush. John Studebaker made wheelbarrows in California and then built wagons and cars. Phillip Armour opened a butcher shop, the beginning of Armour Foods. Levi Strauss opened a dry goods store and later made canvas pants with copper rivets.

LEVI STRAUSS & CO.
SAN FRANCISCO, CAL.
ORIGINAL RIVETED
QUALITY CLOTHING. XX
TRADE MARK
PATENTED MAY 20 1873
Made In U.S.A.
Lot 501

◄ In 1873, Levi Strauss and his partner Jacob Davis first made canvas pants similar to Levi's jeans today.

Boomtowns

From camps to cities

Wherever gold was found, a small settlement called a mining camp grew nearby to serve the miners' needs. Some camps grew so quickly that they became known as boomtowns.

Throughout the gold region, towns grew to provide the miners' food, supplies, entertainment, and other needs. At first the buildings were a combination of tents and wood, but in time more substantial structures were built. A typical gold rush town had stores, banks, saloons, restaurants, barber shops, tailor shops, doctors' offices, lawyers' offices, and—as the town grew more "civilized"—churches. The big day was Sunday, when the miners stopped their work and headed for the nearest town.

► The Wells Fargo company moved gold and other valuables in strong, locked boxes like this one.

City of Columbia

After a gold discovery in 1850, 5,000 people rushed to the site and, within a month, the town of Columbia—above in 1852—was born. At its height, Columbia had a population of 20,000 and was California's second-largest city. With many beautiful brick buildings, it was known as the "Gem of the Southern Mines." Today it is a historic site with a population of around 2,500.

A wagon train brings in food and supplies while a guarded wagon arrives to carry gold out of the town.

GROCERIE

A Population Explosion

When James Marshall found gold, there were about 14,000 people in California—not counting 150,000 American Indians who still lived their traditional lifestyle. Just four years later, in early 1852, the non–American Indian population had reached 250,000! The gold rush was one of the greatest movements of human beings in the history of the world. About one out of every 100 people in the United States headed for California.

Saloons and Hotels

In every mining town, the biggest building was usually a combined saloon and hotel. Not all of them were as attractive on the outside as the one pictured above, but inside many had long mirrors, bright red curtains, handmade wooden chairs, and other furnishings.

Wells Fargo

A big challenge of the gold rush was how to handle lots of gold and transport it to the East. In 1852, Henry Wells and William Fargo opened the Wells, Fargo & Co. office in San Francisco. They bought gold, sold paper bank drafts that were trusted as money, and provided fast delivery of gold and other valuables from California to New York. Wells Fargo offices spread quickly throughout the mining towns of California and other towns in the West.

California becomes a state

At the time of the gold discovery, California was part of Mexico, but that changed a few months later when the U.S. Congress approved a treaty ending the Mexican War. In 1849, a convention representing the citizens asked Congress to admit California as a free state that did not permit slavery. At this time, the spread of slavery to new territories was the biggest conflict in the nation. Congress agreed on a compromise that left other territories open to slavery, and a free California became the 31st state on September 9, 1850. It took almost six weeks for the news to reach San Francisco.

◀ The Wells Fargo office was one of the most important buildings in a gold rush town.

New Finds, New Dangers

Large-scale mining

With so many miners swarming across the goldfields, the easily mined gold on the surface became harder and harder to find. New methods involving new technology developed to harvest the gold deeper within the ground.

Early gold mining in California was called placer mining, from the Spanish word *placer*, a sandbank. This type of gold had been freed from the mountains by erosion and washed down by streams and rivers, where it could be found in free form among gravel, dirt, and sand. After 1852, the placer mining deposits began to dwindle, and two new methods of mining developed. Hydraulic mining used a high-pressure jet of water through a hose to loosen and wash away whole sections of hills so the gold-bearing dirt could be processed. Hard-rock mining involved digging for gold underground to free the gold from the quartz that surrounded it. The placer miners had often formed "companies" with rules and agreements to share what they mined, but these new methods required larger companies with more money. Gold mining became an industry, and a man's daily wages were often the amount he was paid by the company, not the amount of gold he found.

▶ Outlaws watch a wagon train snake through a canyon in the Sierra Nevada.

Using Water Pressure

Hydraulic mining required building a dam to create a strong flow of water that the miners directed at a hill through pipes and hoses. This created massive quantities of gold-bearing "dirt" that was then washed through a series of sluices. Hydraulic mining was outlawed in 1884 because it ruined the environment.

Outlaws and Hold-ups

Although gold was sometimes transported with a wagon train like the one above, Wells Fargo used stagecoaches with the "treasure box" behind the driver and an armed man riding "shotgun" beside him. The most famous California stagecoach robber was a man who called himself Black Bart. He worked alone and robbed about $18,000 (around $500,000 today) from 28 Wells Fargo stagecoaches with an unloaded shotgun!

Hard-rock mining

In nature, gold is usually found with another mineral called quartz. Hard-rock mining is the process of finding deposits of quartz, bringing the quartz out of the ground, and then separating the gold from the quartz. A machine called a stamp mill is used to smash the quartz into smaller pieces, which are then treated with mercury and other chemicals to separate out the gold. Hard-rock mining requires expensive machinery and a large workforce. The greatest hard-rock mining region developed north of the original gold discovery near the towns of Grass Valley and Nevada City. The largest operation, the Empire Mine, yielded 375,000 pounds (170,100 kg) of gold with 367 miles (591 km) of shafts dug 2 miles (3.2 km) deep.

Coyote Holes

Even in placer mining, the richest gold-bearing dirt was often deeper in the ground. Instead of digging deep holes from the surface, miners began digging tunnels called coyote holes into the side of a hill. Some reinforced their tunnels with wood, but others did not and they collapsed.

▶ A stack of silver ingots in Leadville, Colorado, c. 1880

The Comstock Lode

In 1859, gold miners in what is now the state of Nevada found a puzzling bluish rock. When they sent samples to California, they discovered the rocks were rich in silver. A new rush began as thousands of miners crossed the Sierra Nevada to what became known as the Comstock Lode. Between 1859 and 1882, more than $300 million ($8.4 billion today) in gold and silver was taken out of the Comstock.

▲ The mines of the Comstock Lode (shown in this cutaway view) were deeper and more complex than the California mines.

Ghost Towns

Looking for the next big find

When gold ran out in an area, a boomtown could turn into an empty ghost town as quickly as it had grown. Some miners went home to their old lives. Others kept looking for gold.

Mining camps and towns grew wherever gold was found. What happened when the gold ran out depended on the location and the people who lived in the town. Some towns that were on transportation routes turned into small cities. Placerville, for example, the first boomtown near Coloma, survived because it is located near a pass over the Sierra Nevada. It became a stopping point between Nevada and Sacramento, California, for stagecoaches and wagons carrying silver and gold from the Comstock Lode and for Pony Express riders carrying the mail.

Forty-niners Head Home

Hundreds of thousands of gold seekers rushed to California between 1849 and 1852, but many returned home within those same years, some with gold to show for their efforts, others with nothing but disappointment and memories of an adventure. About 90,000 left on ships between 1850 and 1852. However, California kept growing, not with gold seekers, but with men and women who saw new opportunity. By 1860, the "Golden State" had a population of 380,000.

▼ Miners packed up to leave Silver City, Nevada, in the 1870s.

Ghost Towns

Some mining towns were abandoned after the gold ran out. Others hung on to life with a few residents. The largest and best-preserved ghost town of the California gold rush is Bodie, where about 200 original buildings still stand on a windswept sagebrush plain. Today, Bodie is a state historic park. So are Columbia and Coloma—where some people still live and buildings have been fixed up to look like they did during the gold rush.

◄ The town of Bodie, on the eastern slopes of the Sierra Nevada, jumped to life in 1859 when William S. Bodey discovered gold there. It was known for its 65 saloons, street fights, and crime.

Deadwood

After an 1875 gold discovery in a canyon called Deadwood Gulch, the town of Deadwood, South Dakota, grew into the great boomtown of the Black Hills gold rush. It became famous as a Wild West town where gunslinger Wild Bill Hickok was shot and killed while playing poker.

Lifelong obsessions for riches

New generations of prospectors caught "gold fever," too. In 1859, the year the Comstock rush began, gold was discovered in Colorado and about 100,000 gold seekers crossed the plains under the banner "Pike's Peak or bust." In 1863, a gold discovery in western Montana sparked another rush that brought the miners face-to-face with Lakota and Cheyenne warriors. A gold discovery on Lakota land in the Black Hills of South Dakota in 1874 escalated the conflict and led to the defeat of George Custer and his men at the Little Bighorn in 1876.

Shattered dreams

Possibly the biggest losers in the California gold rush were the two men who started it: John Sutter and James Marshall. Soon after the discovery, Sutter's workers left to search for gold and there was no one to harvest his crops. Gold seekers lived on his land, stole his horses, and butchered his cattle. In 1849, his adult son arrived from Switzerland and sold his father's fort to pay off his debts. Marshall did a little mining without much success and retired to a cabin in Coloma near the site of his find.

Klondike Stampede

Gold in the frozen North

THE FIRST BIG "FIND."

In the relentless search for gold, prospectors made finds throughout Alaska, British Columbia, and the Yukon, but none was as big as the Klondike discovery.

On August 17, 1896, an American Indian named Skookum Jim and his white friend George Carmack found rich deposits of gold in a creek that flowed into the Klondike River in the Yukon, a wild region of northwestern Canada. Local miners swarmed to the site, renaming it Bonanza Creek and taking out loose placer gold just as the first prospectors had done in California. The real riches were beneath the surface in glittering seams of gold called a pay streak. The richest deposits of all were on nearby Eldorado Creek. Almost all of the first 40 claims on Eldorado produced $500,000 or more in gold.

▲ This steamboat leaving the port of St. Michael, Alaska, carried gold seekers to the Yukon, a trip of more than 2,000 miles (3,220 km).

Call of the Wild

Twenty-one-year-old Jack London (above) arrived in the Yukon in the fall of 1897 and staked a claim on a creek south of the rich Klondike discovery areas. He spent the winter in a friend's cabin, where he listened to stories told by old prospectors. Although London never found gold, his experiences provided inspiration for two of his greatest books—*The Call of the Wild* and *White Fang*, about men, dogs, and wolves in the far north.

▲ Prospectors make the steep climb toward the Chilkoot Pass, bound for the Klondike goldfields.

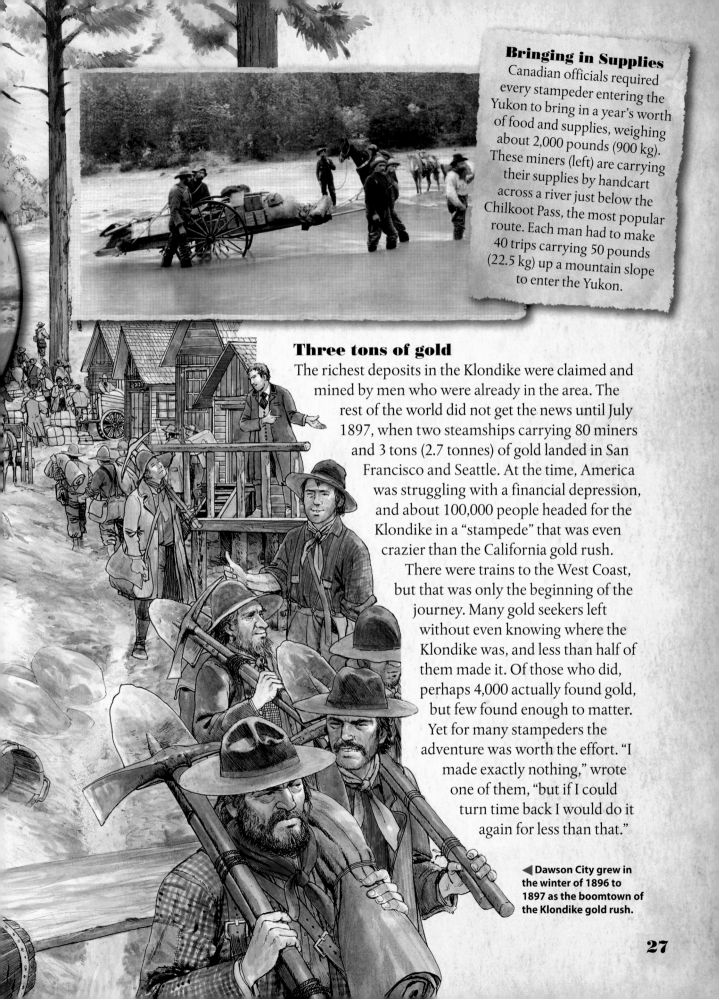

Canadian officials required every stampeder entering the Yukon to bring in a year's worth of food and supplies, weighing about 2,000 pounds (900 kg). These miners (left) are carrying their supplies by handcart across a river just below the Chilkoot Pass, the most popular route. Each man had to make 40 trips carrying 50 pounds (22.5 kg) up a mountain slope to enter the Yukon.

Three tons of gold

The richest deposits in the Klondike were claimed and mined by men who were already in the area. The rest of the world did not get the news until July 1897, when two steamships carrying 80 miners and 3 tons (2.7 tonnes) of gold landed in San Francisco and Seattle. At the time, America was struggling with a financial depression, and about 100,000 people headed for the Klondike in a "stampede" that was even crazier than the California gold rush.

There were trains to the West Coast, but that was only the beginning of the journey. Many gold seekers left without even knowing where the Klondike was, and less than half of them made it. Of those who did, perhaps 4,000 actually found gold, but few found enough to matter. Yet for many stampeders the adventure was worth the effort. "I made exactly nothing," wrote one of them, "but if I could turn time back I would do it again for less than that."

◀ Dawson City grew in the winter of 1896 to 1897 as the boomtown of the Klondike gold rush.

Mining America's Riches
Silver, coal, iron, and black gold

Although gold drove the great mining rushes of the 1800s, there were also silver rushes to Nevada, Arizona, and New Mexico. In the 1900s, the natural resource that created a frenzy was oil or "black gold." It is still one of America's most valuable fuels.

In 1748, the first commercial coal mine began operations in Virginia. Over time, people found many uses for the black rock, including heating their homes, powering locomotives, and producing electricity. Today, coal is mined in 25 states, and the United States is second to China as the world's leading producer of coal. One mineral also important to the growth of the nation is iron, which is used to make steel. Iron ore was first mined in 1847 in the Upper Peninsula of Michigan near Lake Superior. Later in the 1800s, vast deposits were found in neighboring Minnesota. Like gold and silver mines, coal and iron mines drew miners from around the world and led to new boomtowns.

▲ Coal lumps

▼ Boys as young as ten years old were employed at the mines to separate coal from other rocks.

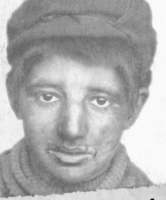

The Cost of Coal

The men in this 1879 image (right) were lucky to be rescued from a mineshaft that caved in. Some mines filled with water or deadly methane or carbon monoxide gas. Many longtime miners developed potentially fatal black lung disease from breathing coal dust. Today's coal mining methods are safer, but there are still fatal accidents.

◀ One of the first uses of oil—in the form of kerosene—was as a fuel for lamps.

◀ The first oil well, drilled at Titusville, Pennsylvania, in 1859

Company Towns

As mining operations became big business, a "company town" usually developed near the mines. The town included small houses and cottages for the miners and their families, and a company store—where food and other goods at high prices were given to the miners on credit, which kept them in debt to the company.

The search continues

Gold, silver, coal, iron, and oil are just a handful of the many important resources mined within the United States. With new technologies and the economic expansion of countries such as China and India, the demand for these resources is rising faster than ever. Today, the U.S. Geological Survey is committed to determining where and how to mine the most important metals without damaging the environment. The biggest fuel issue now facing the country is how to produce more oil while also reducing the use of oil. The largest deposits of oil are in the ocean off the U.S. coastline, and there is a great debate over trying to balance the need for oil against the protection of the ocean environment.

Oil—the New Boom

The modern American oil industry began in 1901 on a Texas hill called Spindletop, where drillers hit a "gusher" that shot oil 150 feet (46 m) into the air and produced more oil than had ever been seen in the world before. An oil boom began, and oil replaced coal as the fuel for ships, trains, and new inventions such as the automobile.

Glossary

assay a chemical test to find the purity of a sample of precious metal

boomtown a town that grows quickly due to economic opportunity

Californios California residents of the 1800s of Mexican or Spanish descent

Cape Horn the southern tip of South America, where the waters of the Atlantic and Pacific oceans meet

cholera a deadly disease caused by a specific bacterium in polluted water

cleats (riffles) ridges that catch heavier gold as gold-bearing dirt is washed over them

clipper ship a narrow, sharp-bowed sailing ship built for speed

emigrants people who leave their homes and travel to another country or another region

forty-niners or 49ers men and women who traveled to California in search of gold from 1849 until 1852

ghost town an empty town

gulch a dry depression in the land where a river or stream once flowed

hard-rock mining crushing gold-bearing quartz to separate out the gold

hydraulic mining using powerful jets of water to remove gold-bearing dirt from the side of a hill or mountain

isthmus a narrow strip of land connecting two large land areas. The Isthmus of Panama connects North America and South America, with the Atlantic Ocean on the eastern side and the Pacific Ocean on the western side

Lakota a powerful American Indian tribe of the northern plains

long tom a long, narrow washing box used to separate gold from rocks, dirt, and other coarse materials

Mexican War (1846–1848) war fought between the United States and Mexico. The United States won and acquired California, Nevada, and Utah, most of Arizona and New Mexico, and parts of Wyoming and Colorado.

mineral a natural solid substance

mint a place where coins are made

placer mining removing loose gold from sand, gravel, or soil

plains the open grassland area between the Mississippi and the Rockies

rocker (cradle) a small, rectangular washing box that was rocked back and forth to separate gold from coarser materials

saloon a place where beer, whiskey, and other alcoholic beverages are sold

settlers people who come from one area and set up home in another area

Sierra Nevada a rugged mountain range that runs north to south through the heart of California

sieve a metal plate with holes to allow smaller materials to pass through while capturing larger materials

sluice a series of long, narrow boxes filled with water used to process large amounts of gold-bearing dirt

tailrace the back end of a ditch through which water flows after turning a wheel for a sawmill, flour mill, or other milling operation

wagon train group of covered wagons that traveled to the West together

Timeline

1799 Gold discovery in North Carolina sparks first, small U.S. gold rush

1839 John Sutter arrives in California

1841 The first organized wagon trains head for Oregon and California

1846–1848 The United States and Mexico fight the Mexican War, and California becomes part of the United States in 1848

January 24, 1848 James Marshall discovers gold at John Sutter's sawmill at Coloma

1848–1854 Main years of the California gold rush. Nearly 500,000 people arrive in California

1849 John Sutter's land is sold as Sacramento grows into a busy city

1850 California becomes the 31st state

1854 Sacramento becomes the capital of California

1856 The first overland mail service to California begins. Mail travels by stagecoach

1859 Silver is discovered in an area called the Comstock Lode in Nevada, triggering a rush to Nevada and ending the California gold rush. A gold discovery in Colorado sparks a new rush across the plains

1861–1865 The Civil War rages in the United States

1863 Gold is discovered at Alder Gulch in western Montana, which develops into one of the richest mining districts in history

1869 The transcontinental railroad connects California with the eastern United States

1874 An army expedition led by George Custer discovers gold on Lakota land in the Black Hills of South Dakota

1876 Custer and about 210 of his men die at the Battle of the Little Bighorn

1877 A rich silver find in southeastern Arizona starts a new rush and makes Tombstone a boomtown

August 17, 1896 Skookum Jim and George Carmack discover a rich deposit of gold in the Klondike region of Yukon, Canada, sparking the last great gold rush, called the Klondike stampede

January 10, 1901 Drillers find a huge deposit of oil at Spindletop, Texas, setting off an oil boom

Information

WEBSITES

For the official websites of the gold rush state historic parks below, go to **www.parks.ca.gov** and select "Visit a Park" in the upper-left-hand corner of the tool bar. Then click on the first letter of the park's name, and click on the park you want. The websites listed below are excellent independent sites.

Bodie State Historic Park
www.bodie.com

Columbia State Historic Park
www.columbiacalifornia.com

Empire Mine State Historic Park
www.empiremine.org

Marshall Gold Discovery State Historic Park
www.coloma.com/gold/marshall-park.php

Sutter's Fort State Historic Park
www.pashnit.com/roads/cal/SuttersFort.htm

BOOKS TO READ

Landau, Elaine. *The California Gold Rush: Would You Go for the Gold? (What Would You Do?)* Berkeley Heights, NJ: Enslow Elementary, 2010.

London, Jack. *The Call of the Wild; White Fang; and To Build a Fire.* New York: Modern Library, 1998.

Raum, Elizabeth. *The California Gold Rush: An Interactive History Adventure* (You Choose Books). Mankato, MN: Capstone Press, 2008.

Schanzer, Rosalyn. *Gold Fever! Tales from the California Gold Rush.* Washington, DC: National Geographic, 2007.

Stanley, Jerry. *Hurry Freedom: African Americans in Gold Rush California.* New York: Crown Books, 2000.

Walker, Paul Robert. *True Tales of the Wild West.* Washington, DC: National Geographic, 2002.

Index